How to Make Your Board Dramatically More Effective, Starting Today

A BOARD MEMBER'S GUIDE TO ASKING THE RIGHT QUESTIONS

Congratulations on your
successful completion of

LeadershipUnited

United Way of Central Indiana

This book belongs to: _____

THE GOLD STANDARD IN BOOKS FOR NONPROFIT BOARDS

Read each in an hour • *Quantity discounts up to 45 percent*

Fund Raising Realities Every Board Member Must Face
David Lansdowne, 112 pp., $24.95, ISBN 1889102326

Nearly 100,000 board members and development officers have used this book to help them raise substantial money – in sluggish and robust economies. Have your board spend just *one* hour with this classic and they'll come to understand virtually everything they need to know about raising big gifts.

Asking Jerold Panas, 112 pp., $24.95, ISBN 1889102350

It ranks right up there with public speaking. Nearly all of us fear it. And yet it's critical to our success. *Asking for money.* This landmark book convincingly shows that nearly everyone, regardless of their persuasive ability, can become an effective fundraiser if they follow Jerold Panas' step-by-step guidelines.

The Ultimate Board Member's Book
Kay Sprinkel Grace, 120 pp., $24.95, ISBN 1889102393

A book for *all* nonprofit boards: those wanting to operate with maximum effectiveness, those needing to clarify exactly what their job is, and, those wanting to ensure that all members are 'on the same page.' It's all here in jargon-free language: how boards work, what the job entails, the time commitment, the role of staff, effective recruiting, de-enlisting board members, and more.

The 11 Questions Every Donor Asks
Harvey McKinnon, 112 pp., $24.95, ISBN 1889102377

A watershed book, *The 11 Questions* prepares you for the tough questions you'll inevitably face from prospective donors. Harvey McKinnon identifies 11 such questions, ranging from "Why me?" to "Will my gift make a difference?" to "Will I have a say over how you use my gift?" And the suggested answers are illuminating.

How to Raise $1 Million (or More) in 10 Bite-Sized Steps
Andrea Kihlstedt 104 pp., $24.95, ISBN 1889102415

How hard is it to raise a million dollars? Easier than you might think, says Andrea Kihlstedt. It's a matter of simplifying the process. Do that and you expel the anxiety. And what seemed impossible becomes doable. Kihlstedt prescribes 10 bite-sized steps. And with nearly three decades of experience and scores of campaigns to draw from, she has plenty of street cred.

The Fundraising Habits of Supremely Successful Boards
Jerold Panas, 108 pp., $24.95, ISBN 1889102261

It's a safe bet Jerold Panas has observed more boards at work than perhaps anyone in America, all the while helping them to surpass their campaign goals of $100,000 to $100 million. Funnel every ounce of that experience and wisdom into a single book and what you end up with is *The Fundraising Habits of Supremely Successful Boards*, the brilliant culmination of what Panas has learned firsthand about boards that excel at the task of resource development.

Emerson & Church, Publishers
www.emersonandchurch.com

HOW TO

Make Your Board Dramatically More Effective, Starting Today

A BOARD MEMBER'S GUIDE TO ASKING THE RIGHT QUESTIONS

Revised and Expanded Edition of
How Are We Doing?

Gayle L. Gifford

Emerson
& Church
PUBLISHERS

First printed January 2012

10 9 8 7 6 5 4 3 2

Printed in the United States of America

Copies of this book are available from the publisher at discount when purchased in quantity for boards of directors or staff.

This text is printed on acid-free paper.

Emerson & Church, Publishers
15 Brook Street, Medfield, MA 02052
Tel. 508-359-0019 • Fax 508-359-2703
www.emersonandchurch.com

Library of Congress Cataloging-in-Publication Data

Gifford, Gayle L.
  How to make your board dramatically more effective, starting today : it's all about asking yourself the right questions / Gayle L. Gifford.
       p. cm.
  Includes index.
  ISBN 978-1-889102-45-0 (pbk. : alk. paper) 1. Nonprofit organizations—Management. 2. Boards of directors. 3. Corporate governance. I. Title.
  HD62.6.G475 2011
  658.4'22—dc23
                              2011023497

DEDICATION

"In a gentle way, you can shake the world."

–Mohandas Gandhi

I've spent most of my life working in and volunteering for nonprofits. It has been a calling for me, and I can't imagine my life's work having taken shape in any other way.

There is much to improve among nonprofit boards. Because the work is so important to the people we serve, we hold high standards for board performance.

Yet it's easy to forget that directors of charitable organizations do what they do without expectation of monetary reward. Heck, most are lucky to get their mileage reimbursed!

While we grasp for the stars, there is much to celebrate. Voluntary philanthropy brings us PTAs, youth sports leagues, music, theatre, dance, therapeutic riding, animal rescue, civil and human rights defense, women and children's advocacy, community development, international service, environmental protection, think tanks, universities, preschools, and too many other benefits to name.

To you who share large parts of your lives in service to the rest of us, *thank you* for caring enough to make your communities and our world a more vibrant, peaceful, and joyous place to live.

CONTENTS

Part III: Building a Great Board

INTRODUCTION

"The art and science of asking questions is the source of all knowledge," said American novelist Thomas Berger. We've known that since ancient times, Socrates being a notable advocate.

Your willingness to ask questions – 34 of them, in fact – lies at the heart of your becoming an effective, dare I say extraordinary, board.

Some are easy to answer – Has each of our directors made a gift? Others are more challenging – Does our vision matter? But all of them are essential questions you must ask, and answer, if you want your organization to flourish.

I mentioned Socrates. Well, the word philanthropy, derived from its Greek root, means "love of humankind." It embodies the best of humanity – voluntary acts of service for the common good.

Today most people practice philanthropy by volunteering or giving through a special class of organizations called *nonprofit*. This book focuses on a specific type of nonprofit, public charities (see the glossary for more information).

The name reflects the idea that no private person or group owns the wealth and property of these organizations. Unlike the case with for-profit businesses, no individual stockholders associated with a nonprofit should have their personal balance sheets enriched by that affiliation.

In exchange for delivering the public benefits for which they're established, nonprofits are accorded a host of privileges, including:

• They don't pay taxes on much of the income they receive.

• Many can accept tax-deductible contributions, which gives people greater incentive to support them.

• They can use the unpaid services of volunteers and not run afoul of labor laws, unlike for-profit businesses.

In a for-profit corporation, shareholders are the owners and elect the board to act in their interests. But in a nonprofit enterprise, where there are no individual owners, whom does the board represent?

A way to think about ownership at nonprofits is that they're owned communally, by society as a whole. And you, the board, represent those owners.

To ensure that these special organizations deserve these special privileges and meet their moral and legal responsibilities, they are entrusted – thus the word *trustee* – to their boards.

Which brings me to you.

You and your board have a legal and an ethical obligation to take the best care of the organization you serve while you go about achieving the purpose for which it was founded. The law calls this charge your *fiduciary* responsibility.

The decisions you make while carrying out your duties can and often do affect people's lives dramatically. In other words, this is serious business.

With such responsibilities to shoulder, you might expect to undergo hours of rigorous training – a sort of director's ed to help you steer the proper course.

In reality most of us learn on the job. If you get any training, it's likely to be a workshop or two on fundraising or basic duties, not a thorough look at the full scope of board work.

The problem is, if you and your board colleagues don't share a common understanding of the work you must do, it can be difficult to judge just what kind of job your board is doing.

This book is an attempt to change that. In my view, your performance as a board is measured against three yardsticks:

1) How will you make the community better?
2) How good a steward are you?
3) How well do you work as a team?

You've chosen to devote yourself to an important cause. What you deserve in turn is the opportunity to experience the extraordinary joy of philanthropic service. This book is designed to help you do just that.

.

Part I

MAKING OUR
COMMUNITY BETTER

"No pessimist ever discovered the secrets
of the stars, or sailed to uncharted land,
or opened a new doorway for the human spirit."

– Helen Keller

1

Does Our Vision Matter?

Imagine those first days of your organization – your founders huddled around a kitchen table, perhaps. There was passion and excitement in their voices as they described the world as it could be.

They were, in all likelihood, committed to big dreams...

- Feeding people who were hungry.
- Healing those who were sick.
- Restoring what had become polluted.
- Bringing music where there was silence.

Your founders imagined a better world and believed in their ability, maybe even obligation, to make it happen – or give it their best. If today you polled your fellow directors and asked them why they serve, would they echo the fiery passion of the founders' vision?

Or would they talk about their board work in mundane terms – attending meetings, overseeing the finances, supervising the CEO?

How did board work get so small? When did directors trade a burning need to right wrongs for arguments over the cost of printing?

Certainly there's a need to outfit and command a tight ship. But that ship has to deliver its passengers to their desired destination, or you've failed to accomplish your mission.

Ultimately, your performance as a board isn't judged by the health of your balance sheet or the square footage of your facility, no matter how important these elements are.

The true measure is the difference you make – call it your vision, mission, or true calling – in the lives you save, the natural resources you protect, the beauty you enhance, or the spiritual solace you provide.

Achieving *that* vision is what matters.

"Not only must we be good," Thoreau said, "but we must be good for something."

2

Have We Set a Goal For the Good We Can Do?

"How will our community be better because of what we do?"

That doesn't sound like a hard question, but for many boards it's the toughest one to answer. And the most salient.

When asked to set a goal for how they'll enhance their community, many boards hedge. It's tempting to think about your organization only in terms of what you are – a community center or a youth orchestra, for example. Boards adopting that viewpoint judge their effectiveness by limited standards: *Did we conduct a range of interesting programs? Is our building well-maintained?*

But the impact of that community center is much greater than its activities and buildings. It brings generations together. It's a safe space where children and the elderly can thrive. It rekindles community spirit. *These* are the results that matter.

What do you want to achieve for your community? Until you know that, you won't be able to design the best programs to get you there.

One of my former clients, a community land trust, learned the power of that question firsthand.

For many years, the board believed its *primary* purpose was to boost public support for land conservation. Although the land trust had protected five hundred acres in its first ten years, its only adopted goals were to expand membership and host education programs.

Yet the directors were acutely aware that the last few farms and open spaces in their community were at risk from intense development pressures. How, exactly, would more members and more awareness save land? And would the lands' owners wait for these other activities to pay off?

With the prodding of several major supporters, the board shifted their questions to ones of purpose and impact. *"Are we really making a difference?"* they asked. *"Are we doing enough?"*

Their answer was *"We can do more."* The board set a bold new goal – to protect two thousand acres – nearly 10 percent of the community – permanently. They restructured and produced astounding results. In the next four years, the land trust more than doubled its protected holdings, and today has reached its two thousand-acre goal.

Too often boards are reluctant to quantify the community impact they'd like to make, fearing they'll fall short of the goal. Maybe you will. But as Beverly Sills said, "You may be disappointed if you fail, but you are doomed if you don't try."

3

How Well Do We Know Our Community's Needs?

In business, you'd be hard-pressed to convince anyone to invest in your company if you couldn't describe the size, characteristics, and needs of your market. Investors need confidence that managers know what they're doing. They want some assurance that their investments can produce significant returns.

Your community investors expect the same of your organization. As the board, you must know the basics of your core business.

Imagine you were starting an agency to help an influx of refugees to your town. What would you want to know?

You'd talk to immigration officials to find out who was coming – how many, how old, how needy. You'd speak with realtors about housing. You'd visit business leaders to inquire about jobs. You'd talk to school officials about enrollment and special services.

And if you were really thorough, you'd go a step further and study the refugees' culture, traditions, and values.

Understanding the scope of community need is an essential part of every board's work, whether you're a start-up or an established organization. And it can be rigorous, requiring careful planning, plenty of phone calls and meetings, hours of research, and still more time to discuss and agree on what everything means.

"Fine, we'll put the staff right on it," you might say. Tempting, yes, but your constituents – especially would-be donors – want to see and talk to you, the people in charge.

Besides, there are benefits to doing some of the research yourself. You'll spread the word about your organization and discover how others see you. You'll likely enjoy the conversations you have. And, if you're truly fortunate, you'll even identify a promising new donor or director.

4

Do Shared Values Guide Our Practices?

Most of us know the Golden Rule: *treat others as you would like to be treated.*

You don't have to be a church, synagogue, or mosque to benefit from a moral code. Nonprofits, governments, and businesses also rely on values as guidelines for action. The Geneva Conventions set standards for the conduct of nations. Professional associations require their members to sign a code of ethics. Some retailers even post their values for customers to see – for example, *We do not test our products on animals.*

A *values statement* allows a nonprofit to define and codify the shared beliefs that underlie its work. It keeps staff and board moving in the same direction – and away from danger. Imagine the fallout if an environmental group was fined for polluting. Think how the media would lambaste a nonprofit serving people with disabilities if its annual meeting were not wheelchair accessible.

In drafting your own values statement, articulate how you differ from organizations that may appear the same. For example:

Our child care center emphasizes children's independence. Or:

We believe that strict discipline is essential to a child's growth.

Are there spiritual or scientific beliefs that guide your work? Maybe:

Our school upholds Quaker values. Or:

Science grounds all of our actions.

Some vision statements include commitments to inclusion and accessibility:

Our services are open to all in need, regardless of their beliefs.

Others restrict participation:

We do not accept donations that could compromise our independence or integrity.

What is key is that you examine your own organization and identify its bedrock beliefs.

If your organization doesn't have a values statement yet, the process of developing one can be enlightening. Many board members are surprised to uncover differences of opinion on what they thought were shared beliefs.

If you already have a values statement, is it still meaningful? And, most important, are the values reflected in everything you do?

5

Are We Prepared To Respond to a Changing World?

When the polio vaccine made its original charter obsolete, the March of Dimes might have dissolved. Instead, believing that what they'd built could still make a difference, they reinvented their mission to address the greatest risks to healthy babies: birth defects, premature birth, and low birth weight.

Your organization may not experience as dramatic a shift. But consider some of the changes you've personally witnessed in your own community:

- Businesses opening, closing, or merging
- Turnover in political leadership
- Population changes
- Shifts or cutbacks in state or federal spending

A vibrant board stays alert to trends and issues that could affect its mission, its constituents, or the revenues it depends on.

In chapter 3, I mentioned one way you can keep abreast of changes – venture out and talk with people in the community. Their concerns will fuel many a lively discussion at future board meetings or retreats.

But if you want yours to be a great board, keep your ears to the ground year-round by doing one or more of the following:

• Periodically, hold your board meeting at a place that matters to your mission. One of my clients helps parents of premature babies. Every so often the board convenes at the hospital so members can meet the medical staff and see the neo-natal intensive care unit. The board of an environmental group where I worked held a meeting at the local power-generating plant to hear directly from its operators about upcoming changes.

• Invite a community expert to speak at your board meeting. An AIDS service organization might ask an official from the state health department to brief its board on funding changes and emerging health concerns. Follow up with a discussion on how what you learned might affect the future of your agency.

• Consider convening your strategic planning committee year-round. A growing number of boards have adopted this practice. In addition to keeping the plan on track, committee members keep tabs on local conditions and alert the board to changes that might affect assumptions guiding the plan.

• Know what's happening in your state house or in

Washington, especially if your organization depends on government grants and contracts. Directors and staff of state humanities councils gather in the U.S. Capitol every spring for "Humanities on the Hill." They meet Congressional representatives and are briefed on upcoming issues of local and national importance.

• Follow the example of many community foundations and hold public forums where directors can listen to community members and learn from local, state, and national experts.

• Have an annual board retreat to dig deeper into complex issues.

How is your board thinking about tomorrow? Have you developed good radar to sense important shifts in your community or in the resources you depend on?

As poet Mark Strand said, "The future is always beginning now."

6

Do We Think and Act Strategically?

"How do we put a park in walking distance of every American child?"

The Trust for Public Land (TPL) challenged itself with that very question. On its face, the answer seemed pretty obvious: raise money to buy land and set it aside for parks. But the solution, it turns out, wasn't that simple.

TPL's research showed that, although city kids direly needed green spaces, municipal parks departments were unwilling to accept new parks they couldn't afford to maintain. And residents chaffed at the prospect of neglected property in their neighborhoods.

So TPL asked the question at the heart of all strategic thinking: *How can we break through this logjam to achieve our goal?*

Voilà Parks for People, an initiative that makes a compelling case for urban parks, helps cities site and design them, and serves as a catalyst for land acquisition and private and public fundraising.

What strategic thinking does, as shown by TPL, is shatter the tired lament, "We've always done it this way." It searches instead for new solutions. It envisions change and questions sacred cows.

To uncover your own breakthrough strategies, try asking yourself the following questions:

• How can we do more of what makes us successful?

• How can we dismantle or maneuver around barriers in our way?

• What is too farfetched to consider? Is there a way it could happen?

• How can we control our future rather than passively accepting it?

When you think strategically, breakthroughs often emerge, as when hunger advocates created elaborate networks to recover wasted food and deliver it to the hungry. Or when environmentalists created the smart growth movement that couples the conservation of rural areas with city revitalization.

Strategic thinking isn't something you do every few years. It's a mindset, a perspective, a way of seeing the world that flourishes when you practice it year-round.

7

Do We Know If Our Programs Are Having An Impact?

With charitable contributions now in the hundreds of billions, a movement is afoot to help define the return that donors are realizing on their philanthropic investments.

Now everyone – government, private funders, and the public – wants to see proof of your results. How much community impact are you having? How do you know you're really creating social change?

This push for accountability is healthy, no doubt. But demonstrating results isn't a simple undertaking for many organizations.

It's much easier, for example, to tally the number of people whose blood pressure was checked than it is to show how lives are enriched by attending your concert or touring your museum.

Consider the firestorm around educational testing in

the public schools. Taxpayers are asking: Are we getting the best return for our investment? Do we know schools are really preparing our kids?

Trying to measure success in our schools has forced us to ask hard questions: What do we want our kids to know and be able to do? Do we only measure math and reading? Does anything else matter, such as life skills or music or sports? Whose kids are being left behind?

Whatever you think about testing, it has certainly changed the conversation concerning the role of public education.

Here's another example.

For three decades, Rhode Island's Save The Bay has been championing a clean and healthy Narragansett Bay. And partly as a result of their work, sewage and toxic pollution have fallen significantly.

But although the water may look cleaner, pollution levels aren't a complete measure of ecological vibrancy. Save The Bay's board wanted to know if the bay was actually healthier.

After considerable deliberation and hours of work, the organization developed a State of the Bay report that measures the bay's ecological health in ten areas, ranging from eelgrass to fisheries. Now the board has a helpful tool to shape priorities and spotlight new problems as they emerge.

If your board hasn't examined your organization's impact, try stimulating interest by asking the questions that lie at the heart of any evaluation:

- *What's working?* So you can keep doing the things that produce results.
- *How do we know?* Because as much as possible, your evaluation should be based on evidence, not just one or two appealing anecdotes.
- *What isn't working?* So you can stop doing it.
- *Why is or isn't it working?* So you can learn how to do better.

Today, fewer funders are accepting the claim "We're good at what we do" without seeing hard data to back it up. Don't be surprised if a charity rater such as Charity Navigator soon profiles your impact – or lack thereof – online for all to see.

Although this may sound harsh, the quality of people's lives is often at stake if your programs founder. And wouldn't your donors derive more satisfaction from supporting you – and be even more willing to contribute to your cause – if they knew your organization was genuinely making a difference?

Part II

BECOMING GOOD STEWARDS

"A little neglect may breed great mischief;
for want of a nail the shoe was lost; for want
of a shoe the horse was lost; and for want
of a horse the rider was lost."

–Benjamin Franklin

8

What Kind of Stewards Are We?

So far, we've examined how well you're serving your community. Now it's time to shift the focus to the second part of your job.

Steward is a wonderful word that describes an individual entrusted with the care and management of another person's property or estate.

There couldn't be a more fitting term to apply to your board. As I mentioned in the introduction, as a director you don't own the organization – it "belongs" to the public and community you serve. You are responsible for its care. Thus, you are a *steward*.

So what exactly are you the steward of? Most boards can easily cite assets such as the endowment, buildings, land, and equipment. But what about things that aren't so tangible?

In the for-profit world, reputation, expertise, or brand often contribute more to a business's total worth than equipment or inventory. Recall how a few years back the reputations of several clothes makers were tarnished when it was revealed that they used child labor and sweatshops to manufacture their products. Sales plummeted and earnings tumbled.

Maintaining reputation, expertise, and brand is as important – if not more important – in the nonprofit world as it is in the for-profit arena. Imagine how difficult it would be to achieve your organization's mission if mismanagement lost you your loyal donors, your tax-exempt status, the goodwill of your community, or the accumulated knowledge and expertise of your staff.

The questions in the remaining chapters of part two will help you assess just how good a steward your board has been.

9

Is Our Organization Worthy of Support?

Can your organization pass the Mom test?

Let's say your mother comes to you for advice: *"Dale, you're well off, your sisters don't need my help. I've decided to leave what money I have to charity. What do you think of my giving it to the group you're involved with?"*

When deciding what to say, you would probably consider two questions. The first is likely to be: Is this organization *worthy* of my Mom's money?

If your group has focused on your mission, there should be little doubt in your mind. As suggested in chapter 3, you already know how much your community needs your organization. You're measuring your impact as chapter 7 recommends. Further, people outside the organization can testify to the importance of your work. Your peers consider your programs a model to imitate. That's all in your favor.

But, although worthiness is essential, it still isn't enough to meet the Mom test. You can probably think of a few worthy causes where you question just how efficiently they operate.

Which brings me to the second Mom question: Is this a place my mother can *trust* with her money?

Trustworthy organizations deliver on their promises. They accept nothing less than ethical behavior. They are open, honest, and aboveboard. Their directors and staff consistently act in the best interests of the community and the people they serve. And they spend their money as their donors intended.

In other words, exemplary organizations combine worthiness of cause with trustworthy behavior.

So lead with your mom in mind. If your organization isn't worthy of her support, it isn't worthy of anyone else's either.

10

Do We Have the Best CEO for the Job?

Have you ever faced a problem at work that everyone was convinced couldn't be solved? Then a new supervisor was hired, and suddenly those seemingly insurmountable barriers vanished.

That's the difference the right person can make.

When you consider how much of your organization's success depends on your CEO, it's essential to have the best person in the job.

So what constitutes the ideal chief executive?

Knowledge, skills, ability, and personality are on the list, of course. And I'd underscore the ability to make things happen. But they're not all.

Imagine a technology school that hires a well-known engineer as its head. She wowed the board with her expertise and innovative ideas. But as the board soon learns, the new executive doesn't have the political savvy to get her ideas past the faculty senate or the interpersonal skills to generate alumni gifts.

What made this individual a great engineer, and a terrific interviewee, didn't translate into being a great leader. She lacked what human resource professionals call the right job competencies – the blend of behaviors and actions that allow people to perform in the position successfully.

Whether you're hiring a new CEO or examining the performance of your current one, you'll want to identify which leadership qualities will help your organization thrive. Maybe you need an entrepreneur who can overhaul a moribund program or funding model. Or perhaps you've experienced rapid growth and need a skilled executive to build the systems to sustain it.

Qualities that I personally think are essential in a CEO are a deep-seated passion for the mission, a fervent commitment to your organization's values, the ability to respond to the unexpected, and a heaping dose of self-motivation and self-discipline. I'm with business guru Jim Collins, who says the best people are the ones who "wake up every day, compulsively driven to do the best they can because it is simply part of their DNA."

How can you be sure you've found the right person? You can't, really – only time will tell. But certainly it'll help if you verify – thoroughly and exhaustively – your candidate's achievements in his or her last few positions. And, if you're assessing your current CEO, it's going to take true grit to decide if he or she is capable of leading you where you want to go.

But remember, once you've found the right person, even a superhero would find it hard to spearhead an organization where the board meddles in management affairs, strips the CEO of power and authority, or allows its chair to unilaterally direct what is really management's bailiwick.

Step back and heed the words of David Ogilvy: "Hire people who are better than you, then leave them to get on with it."

11

Do We Regularly Evaluate Our CEO?

You're at a posh restaurant. The waiter arrives and you say, "Bring me something interesting to eat and something cold to drink."

Imagine how disappointed you are when a few minutes later he returns with tripe soup and prune juice. But that's what you get with an imprecise request. It's not completely the waiter's fault.

It's equally unfair to evaluate your CEO against vague or unstated criteria.

A common complaint I hear from CEOs is that they've never had a formal performance review – whether they're new or have been on the job for a decade. No board should shirk its duty like that.

The place to start is by setting yearly performance goals with your CEO. Indicate what results will be good enough and what you would consider outstanding. Be clear about how you'll measure achievement and what the connection will be between performance and compensation.

Because your CEO's leadership in the office and in the community is so important, remember to set expectations in those areas as well. Hold your CEO responsible for upholding the values discussed in chapter 4. Describe what good relationships with constituents should look like. For example, the Community Foundation of Northeast Alabama wants their CEO to:

> *Establish a strong working relationship with the professional advisor community.... This involves not only creating visibility and credibility for the Foundation within the professional community, but also developing demonstrable working relationships with this group.*

Put all of your expectations in writing. They can be in the form of a business plan, a job plan, or any tool that reinforces the idea that the evaluation will be based on specific criteria, not individual opinions.

Also, if the conversation about expectations takes place between the CEO and the board chair or a small committee, remember to ask the full board for its endorsement so that everyone is working from the same set of expectations.

When the designated time rolls around, you owe it to your CEO to complete that formal review. Appoint a small task force to conduct the evaluation. Gather examples from nonprofit colleagues whose CEOs and boards you admire. Because personnel matters can sometimes become litigious, it's wise to get expert advice on the design of the process.

Every organization handles the evaluation of its CEO differently, but here are some key steps to keep in mind:

- Start by designing questions based on the job and leadership expectations you created.

- Gather input from those with firsthand knowledge of your CEO's performance, such as selected board members and senior staff.

- Have your CEO complete a written self-evaluation using open-ended questions designed around the job plan's key responsibilities, annual objectives, and key relationships. For example, "Please rate your performance over the last year in relationship to your job description and your achievement of board-approved objectives." Or "Please rate your performance in identifying, developing, and maintaining relationships with key outside stakeholders."

- Ask your CEO what else he or she needs to lead your organization successfully in the years ahead, such as, "What challenges do you anticipate our organization facing over the next year, and what will you need to meet those challenges?"

- Once you've gathered, interpreted, and summarized the data, prepare a formal document and share the feedback with your CEO. The most useful evaluations use the past as a learning opportunity for future performance and include a professional development plan that outlines new knowledge or skills your CEO may need to acquire to meet future objectives.

After the meeting, you'll want to share the final document, including your CEO's comments and the professional development plan, in executive session with your full board so that everyone understands the expectations that have been set for the future.

And, although a formal evaluation many only occur annually, a healthy partnership between the board and the CEO includes two-way feedback throughout the year.

12

Have We Given Our CEO The Necessary Support?

In the Rumplestiltskin fairy tale, a poor miller's daughter is locked in a room by the king and, upon penalty of death, told to spin straw into gold.

Have you done the same thing with your CEO?

Certainly boards hire their chief executives with high hopes. But mere mortals don't have gold-spinning powers. Still, we seem to expect it of nonprofit CEOs.

I've often heard CEOs, even those who lead revered nonprofits, confess how alone they feel. "I appreciate their vote of confidence," they'll say of their board, "but I'm not completely comfortable steering this ship without some direction."

Surveys show that most CEOs love their work. Yet they also lament that they're subject to constant stress, especially financial and personnel worries. Their days stretch on, evenings are filled with meetings, and let's not forget Saturday's Big Gala.

So when CEOs turn to their boards, they yearn for wise

counsel and the support of collegial, dedicated partners. Too often, they get micromanagers instead ("D'you think we could get some better party favors?"). Or, just as bad, disinterested or unreliable directors who squander their time.

So how can you be a valuable partner to your CEO?

Think about what you would you want from your board if you were in the CEO's shoes. Of course, there are the obvious needs of any staff member – reasonable compensation, a healthy workplace, and opportunities for professional growth.

But what else might you personally want from your board – prompt feedback or well-informed colleagues?

To lay the foundation for a strong and rewarding partnership, why not ask your CEO directly: *What do you most need from us to make this organization succeed?* If you haven't had that conversation lately, now is a good a time to initiate it.

You'll probably hear that your CEO wants partners who deliver on their promises, a trusted sounding board, and passionate champions who promote the organization's cause to their friends and colleagues.

Who knows, backed up by sturdy board support, your CEO just might spin that straw into gold after all.

13

Is Our Relationship With Staff What It Should Be?

According to the U.S. Bureau of Labor Statistics, U.S. companies lose an estimated $3 billion a year to the effects of negativity – high absences and turnover, loss of creativity, low morale, and poor customer relations.

Although many choose nonprofit work for its personal fulfillment, these workplaces aren't exempt from everyday stresses. And optimism can take a beating when each day brings more needy clients than you have the resources to handle.

So why add prickly board-staff relationships to the stress?

It may be obvious, but good board-staff relations start at the top. A sour relationship between the board and the CEO will quickly spill over to the staff. It's hard to lead the way enthusiastically when you're unhappy in your own job.

But there is more you can do to foster good relationships with staff beyond creating a collegial partnership with your CEO.

At many organizations, staff lends support (with the blessing and encouragement of the CEO) to such board committees as strategic planning or finance. Or directors may work directly with staff on special events or government relations.

In large organizations, many staff might not have the chance to work with directors. So you'll need to find other ways to connect, such as attending annual events that celebrate staff milestones. Some boards make a practice of sending the board chair to brief the entire staff personally on major decisions. Also, otherwise routine annual meetings can be transformed into special occasions when directors and staff have opportunities to socialize.

Showing up in the workplace gives you an excellent opportunity to say hello to staff informally and to see firsthand what's happening in your organization. There is a caveat, however. When directors work closely with staff, it's easy to forget you aren't their boss; the CEO is. It's up to you to be disciplined about the limits of your director role.

Staff will always appreciate a board that takes notice of their accomplishments. You can, for example, with the CEO's support, acknowledge years of service or a particularly tough assignment by issuing a formal board thank you or letter of appreciation. I personally am a fan of handwritten congratulatory notes from the board chair.

Overall, the Golden Rule works pretty well as a guideline for board relations with staff.

14

Does Our Board Focus on The Financial Data That Matter Most?

Which of the following describes your board when finances are discussed?

A) Directors scrutinize every line item and grill the CEO on any variances.

B) Directors avoid eye contact with the treasurer and think, "I'm really glad Mary understands this stuff."

C) Directors don't worry about a thing because their CEO has the finances under control.

I hope you're thinking, "None of the above," because the preferred answer is:

D) Directors review a concise report of key financial targets, raise questions about variances, and persist until they're satisfied corrective action will be taken.

Most of us have a love/hate relationship with things financial. We love money but hate the thought of managing it.

How many of us stick to household budgets or follow long-term investment plans (or even have such things)? And reading corporate financial reports – ugh, I'd rather eat roasted cricket! Unfortunately, what may be acceptable in your home isn't sufficient to carry out your fiduciary responsibility as a board.

Although you needn't be a certified public accountant to understand nonprofit finances, you do need to know enough to ask and answer the questions that matter.

When I worked at an international children's charity, our board used a handy tool to hone in on the most important financial indicators. We called it a *top line report*, others use the term *dashboard*.

Each month, rather than scan pages and pages of financial data, our directors reviewed a single sheet on which ten indicators were listed. Every director, regardless of financial acumen, could see at a glance whether or not our $25 million organization was on target.

If an indicator was off, staff attached a report explaining what action was underway to address the problem. Full data was still available as a backup for directors who wanted it.

Of course, the reason for knowing your financial condition is so you can act promptly to keep your organization solvent. Identifying the problem only means something if you take steps to remedy it – wishful thinking won't fill your coffers or trim expenses.

Or, as Eleanor Roosevelt said, "It takes as much energy to wish as it does to plan."

15

Have We Built a Secure Financial Base?

Too many nonprofits operate on a financial tightrope. For some directors, financial planning causes discomfort. Others conveniently entrust all things financial to their CEO.

But the boards of financially vibrant nonprofits – even those with numerically challenged directors – are in the habit of asking simple but shrewd questions:

1) *Do we have enough cash to pay the bills?*

More than a few organizations – for example, those with grants coming due – have months when they can't meet payroll or pay vendors. A simple cash flow budget warns you in time to prepare solutions to these temporary fluctuations. An operating reserve will smooth out the rough spots without sending you running for a line of credit.

2) *Will our income cover our expenses?*

As the board, you have a duty to approve only

budgets that are based on realistic assumptions. And ultimately it's up to you to raise the alarm and mandate corrective action when unanticipated costs will cause a deficit. If you routinely fund annual shortfalls from your reserves, you'll be out of existence in a few short years.

3) *Do we honor donor intent – have we done what we said we'd do with the money?*

Many donors would rather give to a specific activity than contribute for general support. When you solicit money for a particular purpose, say, to fund scholarships for inner-city youth, you make a promise you have to keep. Responsible boards differentiate restricted obligations from other cash needs.

4) *Have we paid our taxes?*

Nonprofit organizations are always liable for payroll taxes. Some incur sales, property, or income taxes as well. Although it's tempting to balance the budget with money owed the tax collector, too many organizations are paying sizable penalties, and back taxes, because the IRS discovered discrepancies in their employee withholding.

5) *Have we saved for a rainy day?*

Some directors mistakenly believe charities can't accumulate a surplus. But wise boards ensure that there are sufficient reserves to manage cash flow or weather emergencies.

How much reserve should you have? Although a

number of experts suggest banking enough to cover a year's worth of expenses (don't laugh), most small organizations would be thrilled to have three months of unrestricted funds in reserve.

Although it isn't easy, one way to build your cushion over time is to make *transfer to reserve* a line item in your annual budget (and have the discipline to fund it, of course).

Your board could ask additional financial questions ("Does our spending match our priorities?" "Have we invested in our future success?"), but the five cited here make a good starting point for building a secure financial base.

16

Do We Report Our Finances Accurately to the Public?

When the finances of energy giant Enron and other major corporations turned out to be smoke and mirrors, publicly traded companies were saddled with tough new federal rules regulating their accounting practices. But even without government regulators snapping at its heels, a trustworthy board will make sure its financial statements are in order.

No one's disputing that you chose your treasurer, chief financial officer, or CEO because of their integrity. Yet think of how disheartening it would be to discover that a trusted colleague cooked the books. So heed the words of the late Ronald Reagan – "Trust, but verify."

The most common way to verify your fiscal situation is by commissioning an annual audit.

An audit will ensure confidence in the numbers you report to the IRS on your annual return (IRS Form 990, 990-N, 990-EZ, or 990-PF; each of these forms, incidentally, is a public document you must disclose upon request and is usually available online for anyone to see). For larger nonprofits, the IRS even requires your 990 to indicate if and how your directors reviewed the form before it was filed.

Because accurate financial reporting is squarely a board obligation, many are voluntarily adopting some of the standards required of public companies under the Sarbanes-Oxley Act (the response to the Enron scandal) by placing their audits in the care of a board audit committee.

Under Sarbanes-Oxley rules, audit committees should be made up of members of the board who are independent, that is, not part of the management team or paid consultants for the organization. And at least one of the directors should have financial expertise.

The process starts with the committee hiring an auditor with nonprofit expertise (and who is free of financial ties to the organization) and ends with a meticulous report presented to the board for approval.

Auditors review your financial statements to ensure that they fairly represent your financial situation and meet generally accepted standards. Along the way, they'll alert you to any existing or potential problems in your financial accounting, fiscal controls, or record keeping.

It's customary to have an audit completed at the end of each fiscal year. Your annual revenues may already trigger the need for a full audit (check your state or provincial law to see if this is the case). Also, some funders, including many foundations and the federal government, require audits of their grantees or nonprofit contractors.

If an audit isn't mandatory and you can't afford one, consider paying for a less costly compilation or review. At the very least, periodically hire an accountant to assess how well your internal controls are protecting you from the possibility of fraud or abuse.

With more nonprofits being called to account by taxing or government bodies, no board can afford to be sloppy about financial reporting. With public confidence easily shaken, the bad apples put the tax-exempt privileges of all charities at risk.

17

Are We Getting Accurate Information?

It's disheartening when a scandal hits a charity: "CEO of highly respected social service agency indicted on multiple counts of fraud and mismanagement ... city inspectors find broken equipment endangers children at nonprofit childcare center ...."

Each time I read one of these stories, I ask: What was the board doing? Weren't they aware of these problems?

Evidently not. But there are other boards, equally culpable, that mandate changes yet fail to oversee them.

One group I'm familiar with adopted a highly prudent approach to a proposed major expansion, insisting that staff raise specific amounts of money before committing to each successive phase of growth. With these benchmarks in place, the board approved the plan and turned it over to a dynamic new executive director. The board stopped paying attention as the CEO expanded program costs without meeting the funding benchmarks. Within a few years, the director was gone – and so was the agency.

Responsible boards don't make wishful assumptions. Instead, they create monitoring systems to ensure that affairs are in order.

As to what's involved in setting up a workable system, let me borrow from internationally renowned board consultants John and Miriam Carver.

The Carvers suggest three ways for boards to gain peace of mind:

1) Ask for a report.

2) Inspect for yourself.

3) Have an outsider conduct the inspection for you.

The best monitoring systems use a combination of all three methods. As an example, let's consider your organization's finances.

You're using method number 1 if your CEO provides you with monthly financial statements or completes the dashboard report we discussed in chapter 14. CEO reporting is probably the most frequently used form of monitoring. It works well enough when the board is explicit about the information it wants and if the person delivering the report is leveling with you.

But as common sense dictates, the best way to verify accuracy is to inspect things for yourself – which leads to method number 2. You might delegate a director to examine bank statements or verify that employee payroll taxes were paid on time.

Finally, if you lack the expertise to evaluate, or if you

want an independent review, you may need to use method number 3, the services of an outside expert. You already do this when you hire an accounting firm to conduct your audit or review your internal financial controls.

Monitoring not only guards against abuse but it's the only real way to verify the performance of your CEO, your programs, even the board itself. And considering that your organization is entrusted to you, monitoring its activities and finances is nothing less than your moral and legal responsibility.

18

Have We Managed Risks to Our Organization?

When considering risk, adopt the Boy Scout motto: *Be Prepared*.

Boards are legally bound to exercise reasonable care (known as the *duty of care*) when making decisions for their organizations. Even the best insurance won't protect you when you're negligent.

Needless to say, you can't avoid every risk or foresee everything that could go wrong. You'd never provide services to a client or host an event if you functioned that way.

So instead, protect your organization by adopting a risk-management mindset. You can achieve this goal by following the advice of the Nonprofit Risk Management Center:

- Inventory what might go wrong.
- Plan for how you'll prevent or respond to that potential harm.
- Safeguard your organization from financial ruin in

the event something bad still happens.

The Center groups the risks you face into four categories: people, property, income, and reputation.

These categories provide an excellent framework for developing a risk-management plan.

For example, have you considered the likelihood of your staff, volunteers, or donors getting injured at your gala event? What if someone slips and fractures a leg?

Certainly, you want to verify in advance that you, the venue, and your caterers are sufficiently covered by liability insurance. You'll also want to review safety procedures with everyone working the event. And you might even recruit a roving clean-up crew to mop spills and remove debris.

And what about your property? Are your computer files backed up daily and safely stored off-site or on the Web? Will your insurance cover the costly tasks of retrieving or reentering data in the event your backup plans fail?

Your insurance company, the Nonprofit Risk Management Center, and even professional associations such as the Public Relations Society of America can be instrumental in helping you figure out what to worry about (as if we don't have enough to worry about!) and how to implement adequate safeguards.

19

Do We Prevent Conflicts of Interest from Influencing Decisions?

Fraud or ethical scandals usually occur when directors (or staff) act in their own interests and not for the benefit of their organizations.

Sometimes conflicts arise purely from board inattention or the desire to avoid offending a fellow director. It's tempting, for instance, to forgo outside bids when a director who's also an insurance agent offers to handle your coverage needs. Or the banker. Or the caterer.

You can't eliminate all conflicts of interest, especially in small communities. After all, you've recruited directors because they have connections to constituents you want to reach.

Still, because directors bring their interests with them, you need to have and enforce a written conflict of interest policy spelling out how to deal with real or perceived conflicts.

Typically such policies include:

- What defines a conflict of interest.

- How and when directors (and staff) are required to disclose potential conflicts.

- Whether directors or their families are prohibited from engaging in business transactions with the organization, or if there are conditions under which such transactions could be allowed.

- What practices must be followed to ensure that any such business relationships meet the standard of an arms-length transaction.

To add another layer of caution in evaluating conflict situations, a colleague of mine suggests you use the *New York Times* test. Ask yourself: *How would our organization look to the public if this deal were reported on the front page of the morning paper?*

Avoiding conflicts of interest falls under a larger legal principle known as the *duty of loyalty,* which requires directors to base decisions on what's in the best interest of the organization – not their own interests.

It also obligates directors to safeguard confidential information – for example, not to secretly slip your donor list to another organization.

Part III

BUILDING A
GREAT BOARD

"Talent wins games, but teamwork and
intelligence win championships."

–Michael Jordan

20

How Good Is Our Board?

So far, we've talked about the work your board has to do – making a difference in the community and being wise stewards of your organization.

In the next few chapters you'll evaluate the strength of your board itself and review how well you're working together. But before getting started, let's step back and look at your board overall.

You likely have somewhere between five and twenty directors, perhaps more. They aren't paid, and still they show up for somewhere between three and twelve meetings each year. Your board's combined contribution of volunteer time probably adds up to hundreds of hours every year.

Are you confident you're putting these immense resources to the best use? Do all those hours and all that talent translate to a powerfully positive force for your organization – something it couldn't exist without?

If you went to each of your directors one by one, would they all agree that the hours they toil on behalf of your organization are well spent? Would they describe their experiences as rewarding, important, even exciting?

Imagine a new director gushing to all of her friends on Facebook, as a colleague of mine recently did, "I'm so honored to be recommended and appointed to the [XYZ] board," and having thirty-three of her friends post sincere congratulations back. (I once served on that board and can tell you I felt the same way, even after six years of service.)

Not every board will be nationally prominent or raise millions of dollars. But every board can be competent, enthusiastic, and committed. In the next chapters, I'll share with you what makes high-performing boards so effective.

21

Do We Recruit the Directors We Want and Need?

Business guru Jim Collins, in describing the principles of great companies, advises, "First Who – get the right people on the bus."

When it comes to your board, do you follow his advice? Do you think of each seat as a job only someone specially qualified can fill? If not, you'll likely wind up with a mediocre, disappointing group.

Too many boards work off of an outdated model, filling director slots with generic titles and replaceable people – a lawyer, an accountant, a marketing director – rather than carefully identifying what mix of talent is right for their organizations.

Here's an example of how to do it better.

A small faith-based organization, serving the poor and homeless around the capital city, saw demand for its services grow as the economy faltered.

With few staff, they needed directors who could not only govern well but would also serve as volunteers eager to roll up their sleeves and help get the work done. Currently, the board consisted of elderly, long-serving directors who were tired and ready for new recruits. I was hired to help them revitalize their board.

First, we came up with a shopping list. On it were:
- More connections to downtown residents
- More interplay with the local college
- Inroads into local businesses
- Exposure in the wealthier suburbs
- Improved financial planning and reporting

Our overall goal was a rejuvenated board that included experienced directors, up-and-coming community leaders, strategic thinkers, people who could help increase the organization's visibility and raise more money, and ethnic diversity.

Clear about our needs, we went shopping. And here's what happened:

- We found a well-connected, emeritus professor of marketing who lived downtown. He was already volunteering at the organization's Friday night meal.

- The communications talent came through contacts with a local association of young professionals of color.

- A church recruit agreed to help with fundraising events, as did the mother of a scout who built shelves for their food pantry.

- The next year, with input from the new members, came a financial planner, a local university chaplain who was already a donor, more help with fundraising, younger people, and more diversity.

Among other things, the refreshed board formed a finance committee, undertook a strategic plan, overhauled their online presence, and ramped up their fundraising. At last report, the group was serving ten times as many people a month than they had the prior year. The room was overflowing at the annual fundraising dinner.

Other boards, including yours, can follow this organization's example. What are the critical challenges you face? What skills, experience, and connections do you need to meet them?

Cast a big net. Push timidity aside. Who do you know who matches your wish list? Who do you know who can help lead you to the directors you're looking for?

"Once we rid ourselves of traditional thinking we can get on with creating the future," said the artist James Bertrand.

22

Are We Prepared Enough To Make a Difference?

Supermarkets invest more in training teenagers to run cash registers than most nonprofits do in training their directors.

Too bad, since there's a lot more at stake when the board blunders than when the checkout kid mistakenly overcharges.

Many with great potential, especially young people, have never served on a board before. Even those who have been on other boards are as likely to have picked up bad habits as good ones.

In earlier chapters we discussed ways to keep directors abreast of important trends and community changes. So let's talk about what else is needed to prepare directors for board service.

The best preparation starts during the recruitment process. During this time, candidates should come to understand your organization and what they're signing on for.

At a minimum, board candidates will need an overview of your organization's history, current activities, and upcoming challenges. They'll need to know what's expected of directors and what specifically you want each of them to do.

Especially helpful will be a site visit. Let board candidates see your programs firsthand and observe a board meeting in action. Include an interview with the CEO and key staff with whom the candidate will be working.

Once on board, your new directors will benefit from a formal orientation program. Typically, it's here that new directors receive the board handbook, a binder containing your bylaws, mission, values statements, budget, policies, and more. Have them sign for it to reinforce its importance and your expectation that directors will come to meetings prepared.

At the orientation, new directors can meet committee chairs and hear about particular projects before choosing assignments. New directors can also benefit from board mentors, to whom they can be introduced at your orientation.

Boards and directors profit further from training throughout the year. Most directors have a great deal to learn about nonprofit organizations generally and your particular issues and community in particular.

Ask current directors what they wished they had known in those first days of service – or what they wish they knew more about now. I know of a charter school's board that asked for a budget workshop and an arts organization's trustees who wanted training on intellectual property rights.

Training may include in-house workshops, seminars offered in the community, site visits, and even self-directed reading and interviews. Not only does this make for better directors, but training in the form of meeting local experts and visiting interesting places is also a wonderful perk of board service.

23

Do We Follow Our Bylaws?

Recently two instances arose in my town that demonstrated the importance of bylaws.

In the first case, a small group of donors attempted to stop the board of a nonprofit library from selling a rare book in its collection.

In the other, the firing of a community action group's popular CEO led to the threat of a lawsuit to nullify the vote and oust the board.

In each case, the disgruntled parties charged that the board had failed to act in accordance with its respective organization's bylaws. How well do you and your fellow directors know the fundamental rules governing your organization?

Although no one expects you to commit your bylaws to memory, it's not unreasonable to expect every director to be fluent in their most important provisions, such as rules for voting, nominations, quorum, or terms of service.

Failure to follow your bylaws can invalidate board

elections, diminish legal protections, or expose you, the other directors, and the organization as a whole to liability. It can also signal that your board isn't taking other responsibilities seriously. If your bylaws are outdated because your practices have evolved, you need to change them. Of course, don't do that simply to solve temporary problems, such as a failure to meet a quorum.

If your bylaws need updating, here are several points to keep in mind:

• Follow your own rules. That is, make sure you follow the procedure in *your* bylaws for changing your bylaws.

• Simplify: Limit your bylaws to the basic board procedures, such as terms of service, elections, quorums, officer positions, and the like. Additional details can be outlined in subsequent board resolutions (see the next chapter), e.g., more complete job descriptions for officers and committees or a detailed conflict of interest policy.

• Enhance flexibility: List the committees required by state law or absolutely essential to board functioning (governance and audit committees, for example). Your bylaws can delegate to the board the ability to create or disband other committees as needed.

• Get an attorney's review: Because your bylaws are a legal document, have proposed changes reviewed by your legal counsel to ensure they say what you intend and that they conform to state and federal law.

The clearer and better organized your bylaws are, the more likely your board can and, more important, *will* follow them.

24

Do We Make Policy Instead Of One-Time Decisions?

Bylaws aren't the only rules governing your organization. Board-voted policies also guide your staff and your own actions as a board.

Effective boards make policy rather than decisions. If that sounds confusing, let me clarify the distinction.

Decisions answer a particular question confronting us here and now. They often lack application to any future questions that might arise.

Policies, on the other hand, provide a decision-making framework that can be applied to current and future questions. Not only are they key to sound decisions but policies also allow boards to delegate authority more effectively.

Here's an example:

Your well-known organization regularly receives offers from businesses interested in marketing opportunities. For example, a local supermarket would like to put your logo on its product and offer you a percentage of the proceeds.

Every time an offer like this arises and the CEO feels unsure about it, he brings it to the board for a decision. Largely because your board's reasons for accepting or rejecting such proposals are based on the likes and dislikes of the directors in the room, each new offer is discussed. Thus, tonight's decision may contradict one you made last month.

This rehashing of similar issues, whether welcomed by the board or forced upon them by the CEO, is inefficient and borders on micromanagement.

Policy making offers a better approach. The board can streamline decision making, ensure consistency, and even delegate more decisions to staff by creating a policy for this type of venture.

In the example above, a cause marketing policy would outline the conditions that must be met before any deal is acceptable (e.g., minimum dollar guarantees, agreed payment schedules, written contracts, use of your organization's name and logo, prohibited businesses or types of deals, and compliance with Better Business Bureau guidelines). Once in place, the next offer can be accepted or rejected by the staff by applying this policy to it.

Of course, policies only have value when they're followed. If the only record of your policies is in the meeting minutes, within a year no one will remember the details – or even if you made a policy at all.

Improve your board memory by incorporating each policy into a policy manual. Arrange the policies by topic, mark them with an adoption date, and tuck them into your board and staff handbooks.

25

Does Our Board Govern and Resist the Temptation to Manage?

The board governs. Staff manages. If only the line were so clear to directors!

In the midst of a detailed committee report, it's always tempting for directors to focus on nitty-gritty details such as what the Web site should look like, or what band should play at the upcoming gala, or how long the fundraising letter should be.

But these aren't decisions to be made by the board, the *governors* of the organization. They're the responsibility of your managers – the staff.

Directors who are chief executives or top-level managers in their own workplaces are accustomed to giving orders. They may have a hard time respecting the boundaries of their board positions. But understanding and observing the boundaries between board and staff roles are key.

Here are steps you can take to reduce the temptation to manage:

• Create formal board policies, as discussed in the previous chapter, which allow you to delegate more effectively and in turn reduce the inclination of any one director to create standards on the fly.

• Keep board meetings focused on questions of major policy importance, such as defining the sustainable business model for the organization, rather than how many direct mail appeals should go out this year.

• Clarify the distinction in your director job description: "When directors offer advice to the staff, remember that staff has the prerogative to accept or reject any advice that doesn't come in the form of a board-approved decision."

• During your board orientation, discuss an example that clarifies the distinction between directors giving advice (allowed when staff ask for it) versus ordering staff around (not allowed at any time).

• Create written descriptions of the role of board committees, with board-approved goals for what they need to accomplish. Be clear about what role staff plays in the committee.

Here's a simple place to start making the distinction: Model the way in your board meetings. When conversation wanders inappropriately into staff territory, any director can pull it back – "It's always fun to talk about these things, but these are staff decisions. Let's get back to board work."

26

Do Our Committees Improve the Functioning Of Our Board?

Draw a line down the middle of a sheet of paper. On the left side, list all of your board's standing committees. Then, on the right side, write down what each committee is expected to accomplish this year.

How did you do?

Directors can usually answer the first question. The second gets to the heart of effective committee use.

Committees work best as mini-think tanks that can summarize particular issues, offer options, and lay out their implications. Great committees improve the effectiveness of the full board without usurping its authority to make decisions.

On the other hand, committees that make decisions that should go before the full board or that allow the board to abdicate its responsibility make your board less effective. Having a finance committee, for example, doesn't exempt the remaining board members from their fiscal responsibilities.

In assessing the need for individual committees, ask yourself the following:

1) *Does this committee make our board more effective?*

2) *Does this committee improve our board deliberations?*

3) *Does this committee help advance our strategic plan?*

4) *Do we really need an ongoing committee, or could this project be completed by a time-limited task force?*

5) *Is this committee still needed at all? Can we dissolve it (in accordance with the bylaws, of course)?*

In addition to your written committee description, it's good practice for the board to assign every committee a set of annual objectives. Some might be routine (*complete CEO performance review*). Others might be special projects (*create a policy for accepting corporate gifts*).

Too many boards have a tendency to proliferate committees unnecessarily. Try limiting standing committees to the fewest needed, using temporary working groups to address short-term assignments. State or provincial law will advise whether you're required to have any standing committees at all.

27

Do We Avoid Rubber-Stamping and Decision-Reworking?

You enthusiastically joined a new task force at work. Your boss shows up for the first meeting, tells you he's met with his inner circle and has come up with a solution for you to approve.

You raise a few questions, but otherwise vote in favor because you don't have much of a choice (short of updating your résumé, that is). Oh, and by the way, you and your task force are 100 percent responsible for any problems resulting from the boss's decision.

How many times would this happen before you stopped volunteering for any new assignments?

Unfortunately, this rubber-stamping scenario plays out at many nonprofit board meetings.

Rubber-stamping happens when the CEO and board chair take unilateral action on big issues and then ask the board to endorse that (already implemented) action. Or when important discussions transpire only in committees and are then reported to the board, with additional discussion discouraged or abruptly curtailed. Or when timid directors are afraid to speak up.

Rubber-stamping is especially frequent in boards with an executive committee.

Designed to act for the board only in emergencies – when the full board cannot be easily convened – too many executive committees have taken on a life as mini-boards where the real action takes place.

With video and teleconferencing readily available, the technical challenges of convening a full board have greatly diminished. Most states allow board action via electronic equipment as long as all directors can hear each other at the same time.

If decisions can wait for a scheduled executive committee meeting, then surely (in all but extraordinary circumstances) they can wait for a scheduled board meeting, especially if the board meets frequently.

You may have a good reason for having an executive committee – perhaps your board is spread across the globe and meets only three times a year – but a growing number of boards are deciding they don't need one.

Whatever you decide, you aren't off the hook for your fiduciary obligation if you let someone else make a decision that is yours to make.

On the flip side of rubber-stamping is decision-reworking. Does your board have difficulty finalizing decisions? Does it keep reopening decisions made meetings ago?

Causes of decision-reworking include poor board attendance, lack of adequate information or discussion, absence of policies, failure of dissenters to speak up, or unskilled meeting leadership.

You can guard against rehashing the same old items by making sure all concerns have been aired and high levels of agreement reached. A good technique for improving agreement on contentious issues is to spend one meeting considering the pros and cons and waiting until the next meeting to vote. This process provides time for directors to think more clearly and give the issue their full consideration.

28

Are Our Meetings Productive?

"Who called this meeting?"
"We thought you did...."
"Maybe meetings have become a life form capable
of calling themselves and reproducing via human hosts."

– From *Dilbert*, by Scott Adams

If you serve on a board, you can't escape meetings. And, unfortunately, it takes only a few bad meetings to drive directors away.

Bad meetings are the ones where some directors dismiss dissenting opinions or where one director dominates the discussion. Some directors think long meetings are a bother; others feel short ones don't allow enough time for discussion.

Regardless of our personal preferences, I think we can all agree on what a good meeting feels like. The lively discussion is about important issues. The chair is a good facilitator. Your opinions matter. You enjoy your colleagues. You leave enthusiastic and willing to help your team achieve its big, bold vision.

If your meetings need repair, here are several strategies that can help:

• *Set up short agendas that focus on weighty topics.* Limit agenda items, and you'll have time to discuss substantive issues. Ignore distracting details and use your dashboard (chapter 14) to focus on key variances.

• *Don't rehash the past.* Banish oral reports about things that have already happened. Put reports in writing to read *before* the meeting. Insist that committees bring well-framed policy questions for consideration. (See chapters 24 and 26.)

• *Adopt practices that improve your deliberations.* Some organizations tackle all big issues in two meetings, one to discuss a topic carefully and one to vote. You may want to rely on the old standby, Robert's Rules of Order. Or an alternative such as Quaker consensus might suit your deliberations better.

• *Bring your mission alive.* My humanities council starts by discussing a short story, poem, or article sent to directors in advance. City Year asks directors to share a "ripple" – a story of an act of courage or belief that has made a difference.

Let me put in a good word for food. I knew a community organizer who once said, "Never throw a meeting when you could have a pizza party." Now, no one's expecting a party, but the pizza part sure sounds good when the meeting is at lunch or dinnertime. It's hard to concentrate over the din of stomach rumblings.

29

Has Each of Our Directors Made a Gift?

No need to equivocate here. Every single director of a charitable organization should make a donation. No exceptions.

You may have heard two common justifications for this stricture:

• Funders, notably foundations and corporations, expect 100 percent board giving.

• Directors can't credibly ask others for money when they haven't made their own gifts first.

These are very good reasons, but I can cite instances where they weren't a factor. Money was raised anyway.

In my experience, there's a third, more pressing reason for you to contribute: unwillingness to give is a pretty reliable sign you don't have passion and commitment for your organization.

Great directors feel the righteousness of the cause, in their head and in their hearts. They take their work seriously and know if they don't do it, no one else will.

Don't misunderstand. Charitable giving is a voluntary act. You can't coerce directors into giving. What I'm suggesting is that when you ask directors to serve, one of the obligations the *right* candidates will readily accept is the act of giving.

Remember the Mom test? Call this the director test.

After all, if your directors, those with the legal and moral responsibility, won't put their money to work for the cause, why should anyone else?

Inevitably, when discussing board giving, the question arises: *Should we mandate a minimum gift amount?*

Since many organizations can benefit from having directors from a wide variety of financial circumstances, it usually doesn't make sense to prescribe a minimum gift level. Each director has a different capacity to give. And if you set a minimum, it's pretty likely that's all you'll get.

If I were pinned down, I'd say ask your directors for a gift that reflects the depth of their commitment and personal financial situation. At a fundraising conference I attended, the CEO of a local children's charity shared that their directors are asked to consider a donation that puts the organization among their two or three most important gifts of the year.

How much to give? As my dear departed colleague Herb Kaplan always said, "Give until you feel good."

30

Have We Decided The Board's Role in Fundraising?

I can't think of another board issue that causes as much consternation as fundraising. Countless books and workshops are devoted to the subject of board fundraising.

Staff members grumble that directors don't live up to their fundraising responsibilities. Directors complain that they never signed up to harangue their friends with requests for money. Both sides blame the other for fundraising shortfalls.

On the one hand, it's commonly held that boards are responsible for raising money. On the other, there's no guarantee that the lawyers, doctors, or professional wrestlers on your board have any fundraising talent whatsoever. You can easily find large and successful organizations – from social service providers that depend on program fees to national advocacy groups that rely on individual contributions – where virtually all the fundraising is done by staff.

The question really is *Do you as the board have an* obligation *in resource development?* Absolutely. It starts with something we've discussed already: building an organization that's trustworthy and worthy of support. Absent that quality, it's nearly impossible to raise money.

But you're also responsible for ensuring that your organization *has* the resources to accomplish its mission. Fulfilling this obligation starts with deciding what funding model will fill the coffers – the types of revenues, how much, and in what proportion.

Being responsible for resources also means deciding *who* is tasked with generating those funds. When it comes to raising income from program fees, government contracts, or tasks requiring specialized fundraising skills – direct marketing, proposal writing, planned giving – most boards delegate these responsibilities to staff.

But if your revenue plan requires more individualized giving, then your CEO or other fundraising staff may need help opening doors to potential funders, whether individuals, business leaders, or even government officials.

Here, directors usually have more standing and clout as volunteers, colleagues, friends, and community leaders themselves.

Of course, you're free to decide that directors aren't obligated to open doors or to raise money, and hand off total responsibility to your CEO. Just be sure that he or she has the staffing, skills, resources, and time needed to meet those fundraising goals without your help.

Or you can work out a reasonable and agreed-upon role for directors that might include making introductions, building relationships, thanking donors, and, yes, maybe even asking for the gift.

But don't lead staff to believe you'll do fundraising if you won't. And don't assume staff will be successful at reaching ambitious fundraising targets without all the tools they need.

Unfortunately, tens of thousands of nonprofit organizations aren't raising much money at all. Could it be they're still arguing over the directors' roles?

31

Do We Have a Way to Evaluate Our Own Performance?

You probably see your physician each year, check your weight periodically, and glance at the mirror several times a day. These are all essential ways to evaluate your health and head off potential problems.

Regular board evaluation is just as essential. Think of it as preventive health care for your board.

There are numerous ways to evaluate your performance: at an annual retreat, at a board meeting, or one-on-one with individual directors. All three make a nice package. Let's discuss each in turn.

Retreats

Many boards review their performance at a special half- or full-day gathering set aside for that purpose. A questionnaire asking directors to rate the board against a number of key indicators – such as the questions in this book – can help guide the discussion. A community foundation head recently said that instead of a *retreat,* his board holds an annual *advance* – I love the concept!

Board meetings

It's best if your board has time throughout the year to discuss its performance. That way, emerging problems can be quickly addressed. Consider reserving some time at a meeting every quarter or semi-annually to review how your board is functioning and how it might improve.

One-on-one

Another important aspect of board evaluation is for the chair to check in with each director, one-on-one, at least once a year. These personal conversations will alert you to any problems and help a non-performing director become active again (or offer him or her a graceful exit from the board).

•••

Of course I think reading this book together is a great way to get a conversation started. And there are a multitude of helpful tools online for you to use. Whatever evaluation method you choose, keep in mind Mae West's admonition: "An ounce of performance is worth pounds of promises."

32

Have We Made Board Excellence Someone's Priority?

Great boards don't just happen. They are created by regular care and feeding.

But who on the board takes on this role of board caretaker? In most organizations, it defaults to the board chair, adding an enormous responsibility to an already demanding job.

In organizations where no one is tending to the board, the CEO usually steps in. This situation isn't desirable, either, because it turns the board-CEO relationship on its head.

There is another solution. Increasingly, organizations are expanding the scope of their nominating committees to include other facets of board development. This reconstituted group, often called a *governance committee*, takes on these additional tasks:

• *Director and board evaluation*. The governance committee can coordinate the annual evaluation of individual directors and the board as a whole and oversee recommendations for improvement (chapter 31). It can ensure that bylaws are followed and term limits observed (you do have term limits, don't you?).

• *Leadership transitions.* Boards that fail to groom new leadership often end up with the least reluctant director as president, instead of an eager and qualified new leader. An untrained or uninterested president can wreak havoc on board functioning. Make your governance committee responsible for preparing the best.

• *Committee development.* The governance committee can help the board determine when to create new committees or when to terminate those no longer needed. It can also nominate committee chairs and help those chairs round out their respective committees with non-board volunteers if necessary (chapter 26).

• *Director education.* Have this committee coordinate new director orientation and the other types of training we've discussed (chapter 22).

Other responsibilities for the governance committee include updating board job descriptions, overseeing board mentoring, or recognizing director accomplishments. I'm aware of governance committees that oversee changes in the bylaws or are responsible for ensuring that departing directors are properly thanked.

Although the governance committee needn't be large, its responsibilities are important enough that it should meet year-round.

33

Do We Appreciate Our Directors for What They Do?

You don't have to be an anthropologist to realize that humans love to join groups. Book groups, motorcycle clubs, listservs, cooking clubs, chat rooms, faith-based organizations, alumni associations, sports teams – you name it, and we'll belong.

In reality, your board is just another group. And when you ask someone to join, you're asking him to choose you over another way to spend his time.

With so many choices and limited free time, why should anyone belong to a group that doesn't bring her joy or fulfillment?

How, then, can you make serving on your board worthy competition for your directors' time?

First, offer meaningful work. That includes board meetings that matter, future-focused discussions, or volunteer opportunities where directors feel they're making a difference in the organization's success.

Then make sure every director knows how deeply you appreciate the work he or she does. A friend of mine says the best appreciation is unexpected and memorable. Here's an example of that from another colleague:

A health problem, coupled with a board disagreement, prompted an extraordinarily hardworking director to cut back her service. But rather than let her fade away, as many boards might do, this board surprised her at an annual gathering with a simple award: her photo blown-up and labeled, "Our Champion."

This special appreciation was enough to rejuvenate the director's passion. Now she's back to her old super-volunteer self.

When deciding on your own forms of recognition, stay with ideas appropriate for your organization. A community garden, for instance, might present directors with the inexpensive gift of basil seedlings.

For its popular Daffodil Day fundraiser, one state division of the American Cancer Society loaned its best-performing local board a striking painting of the flower.

Some groups are even more creative. I've heard of organizations that send letters of appreciation to a director's spouse and kids honoring her sacrifice. What a moving way to communicate gratitude through the people closest to the director! Long after that director's board service is done, she will remember that gesture of appreciation and feel pride, connection, and maybe even ongoing commitment.

Alternately, what happens in the heart of a director who departs without thanks or scarcely any notice? I recently attended an annual meeting where not a word of appreciation was expressed for a director rotating off after six years of service. What mistreatment for someone who very well could be a lifelong advocate and volunteer.

Everyone likes appreciation, and boards that nourish and nurture their directors never lack for candidates for board service. Word gets around.

34

Do We Act with Courage and Conviction?

As a child, I loved *The Wizard of Oz* (I still do). This classic bursts with lessons for all ages:

- No matter how far you travel, there is no place like home.
- Good friends are treasures to cherish.
- There's nothing like common sense.
- Be skeptical of authority.

And for nonprofit boards:

- If you care, you'll find the courage to overcome the impossible.

When you signed up for board service, you took on a rigorous job. One thing the recruiting committee may have forgotten to tell you is that it takes a lot of courage to serve on a board.

Why?

Because boards sometimes have to take on unpleasant tasks, such as cutting budgets that result in staff or service layoffs, or terminating a failing CEO or fellow director.

But even routine board activities can require some pluck, such as . . .

... asking a question – when you're new, or when no one else does. And persisting till you get an answer you understand.

... suggesting it's time to do things differently. Or dissenting, especially when yours is the lone voice.

... reaching out to your friends, family, colleagues, or even strangers to ask for their help, especially if you're asking for their money. And . . .

... critically and honestly assessing your own performance.

You don't have to be extraordinarily brave to be courageous. The Cowardly Lion's courage came from a great team, a strong belief, and a powerful cause. Does this sound like your board?

Just remember, like Dorothy, you don't need a room full of superheroes to accomplish great things.

Just heart ...

hard work ...

and the nerve.

GLOSSARY

Director

Director refers to the official voting members of the board of directors. In some nonprofits, directors may be called *trustees.*

Chair of Board

This term describes the board's top volunteer position. Many organizations use the title *president.*

Because the term *president* is sometimes used to describe an organization's CEO, in this book I use *chair of board* to avoid confusion.

CEO

I've used the term *CEO* or *chief executive officer* throughout the book to refer to the top staff position in a nonprofit. Many call this person the *executive director.*

Nonprofit Organization

Although boards of many nongovernmental organizations may find much of value in this book, I've written it from the perspective of nonprofit organizations known as *public charities* in the United States.

In this country, a public charity is a nonprofit organization that receives tax exemption under section 501(c)(3) of the U.S. tax code. It meets the requirement of having varied sources of support and differs from a private foundation, whose sources of support are relatively limited.

Although there is a growing movement to call

charities by another name, such as *social benefit organizations*, I've stuck with the term that most who are reading this book will recognize, *nonprofits*.

Many of the principles of good governance discussed in this book, however, will apply to any board.

GRATITUDE

Thank you Bonnie Koenig, Mary Jo (MJ) Kaplan, Jonathan Howard, and Andrea Joseph for your early advice and professional wisdom.

Thank you to my colleagues who shared candid feedback on the first edition of this book: Edwin Cancel, Ellen Fineberg, Jane Garthson, Bonnie Koenig, Hank Lewis, Jeff Masarjian, Ken Phillips, and Sarah Richardson.

To my wonderful clients and colleagues: I learn so much from you every day.

A very special thank you to my wonderful spouse, Jonathan W. Howard, for your skilled writer's eye and loving support.

About the Author

Gayle L. Gifford is a provocative writer, respected consultant, creative strategist, and long-time advocate for peace and justice. For Gayle, every nonprofit is a promise to its community, a societal commitment to create a better life full of hope, beauty, promise, and equal opportunity for all.

Gayle believes that each nonprofit has an obligation to deliver on its commitment. In her work, she helps organizations be wise stewards of all of their resources, including their programs, their funding, their environment, and the human beings they touch.

Gayle brings her decades of experience at nonprofits small and large as a founder, director, volunteer, and senior manager to her consulting work with nonprofit boards and staff.

She is a frequent contributor to professional publications and online discussions on philanthropy. She is author of *Meaningful Participation: An Activist's Guide to Collaborative Policy-making*, contributing author to *You and Your Nonprofit: Practical Advice and Tips from the CharityChannel Community*, and co-author of *Bringing a Development Director on Board*.

A mother of three fabulous children, now grown, Gayle can be found enjoying the many pleasures of her adopted state of Rhode Island and its capital, Providence, where she and her husband/business partner make their home.

Visit her Web site or blog, *The Butterfly Effect*, at www.ceffect.com. Or connect on Twitter @gaylegifford.

Copies of this and other books from the publisher
are available at discount when purchased in
quantity for boards of directors or staff. Call 508-
359-0019 or visit www.emersonandchurch.com

Emerson
& Church
PUBLISHERS

15 Brook Street • Medfield, MA 02052
Tel. 508-359-0019 • Fax 508-359-2703
www.emersonandchurch.com